A Twinkling of Stars

by

André Leonard George

DORRANCE PUBLISHING CO., INC.
PITTSBURGH, PENNSYLVANIA 15222

ISBN # 0-8059-6788-5
Printed in the United States of America

First Printing

For information or to order additional books, please write:
Dorrance Publishing Co., Inc.
701 Smithfield Street
Third Floor
Pittsburgh, Pennsylvania 15222
U.S.A.
1-800-788-7654
Or visit our web site and on-line catalog at www.dorrancepublishing.com

Contents

Foreword

In my book, *The Call to Love*, I take the reader from unrequited love to a love that is centered on God.

In this book *A Twinkling of Stars*, I hope to give a bit of the feeling of love I experience in the beauty and magnitude of God.

I hope that it will augment the spiritual journey of both those who are in the midst of God and those who are still searching for spiritual involvement.

André L. George

Creation

By God's design, first there was silence,
then the Big Bang
followed by the many notes of love
that make up the Music of the Spheres,
eventually to join the Symphony of Heaven.

Beauty

The most beautiful places
in the universe
are in our souls
and how we perceive with them
the grandeur of God

On the Journey

Try not to consider, too much, people
by degrees of rudeness of politeness
or savvy, but rather on levels of
spirituality, of which every human
on the planet has room for unlimited growth.

There is no special merit where you
are on your spiritual journey; God can
come and meet you unannounced and
powerfully no matter where you are
on your journey of spiritual growth.

It is important to love and help those
above and below you, in front and
behind you, to prepare you for whom
you might see on the other side of the
destination.

A Twinkling of Stars

I step out into the night. I look up and see
the brightness of the stars, their twinkling
against the black velvet of the sky,
and I can't help but feel that all of infinity
is funneled into this moment, this place
where I stand.
It is only with life, focused and awake
to the present, that we can sense
the magnitude of Heaven,
where even the most delicate of flowers
reveals the awesomeness of the universe.
I thank God that each one of us
has within us the ability
to touch the infinite.

A Heaven Within

One can look up into the summer night sky and
see stars and an infinity of depth in the darkness.
We can close our eyes and see the darkness in
front of us, a darkness not unlike that of the night,
but without the stars. This darkness has a glow,
a light ever changing in form and shape peculiar to
the viewer. When we close our eyes and see this
infinity, we can imagine that somewhere out there,
deep within the expanse, is a place larger than all
the habitable worlds combined. A place called
Heaven. And one day our journey might take us
past this darkness over immeasurable distances and
into the light of Heaven. Let us be reminded that
God has placed Heaven in reach of us all, and a
vision of Heaven is within each of us. For we are
all connected by the Infinite.

I Need Love

There is a voice sounding throughout the world.
It rises amongst the war, the poverty, the starvation.
Sometimes in a whisper to just be taken notice of.
Sometimes so loud it can't be ignored. Moving
people to action. It is the voice of compassion.
The voice of humanity, a humanity that begs for
healing. It is a voice that says, "I love you, I want
to love you, love your neighbor, your brother, your
sister and let this love spread to every corner of the
earth." Let it quell the fires of war, the pain of poverty,
the hunger of starvation. Heed the yell that this world
screams out with: I need love, I need love, I need love.

This Sorrow, This Strength

My heart aches for those who died for the sake of love,
for those who were martyred cruelly, fed to the lions,
tortured because they followed the Path of Love. They
were giants in their faith. Even in their dying, they
strengthened those spared and left behind. For all the
sorrow that was there and remains to this day, there is love,
and where there is love there is strength. A strength that
cannot die to the sword or the bullet or the lion. It is
this strength that the martyrs have imparted to me, this
love, this sorrow. Yet I shudder to the test. Will my faith
ever be as strong as the martyrs? Will my love be a love
that cannot die? I can only pray and live my life with the
strength that love allows.

My Tears of Grief

The drops of tears in my heart act like prisms
for the light of love that shines
in my heart.
The tears cast colors of memory
of all my Lost Ones, my Sorrows,
and fill my soul with rainbows
of hope
that those who have gone before me
are in heavenly glory.

I Love You

When God first breathed life into the world, He breathed it with the words "I love you." Since the dawn of time, those three words have been the most important words in humanity, all nations, all languages. Those three words are felt closest to the soul, deepest to the body. The words "I love you" can bring tears of joy, laughter from the heart, and gladness to the spirit. And it is only the words "I love you" that will one day bring the separate peoples of the world together and together one day sing out an "I love you" to the universe and to God.

From your heart, from your place in humanity, you can begin the song "I Love You." With your voice, with the voice of humanity, we will bring a new sound, a new movement to the Music of the Spheres and to the Heart of God.

Hope to the Stars

I feel that God watches over the earth much like a father watches over his child. And that now the earth is in its late adolescence—rebellious, energetic, wanting to find its own way with newfound freedoms, ability, intellect. Also very troubled, precarious its position. Quite possibly a danger to itself. Yet it is the earth that holds the hope of the universe, for it is here that God has placed man, and amongst men, Jesus, God's only Son, the doorway to Heaven. It is this earth that shouts out to the stars, and if we survive our adolescence we will mature and become the birthplace of a new Heaven, a new earth to shine in glory for all eternity.

The Music of the Stars

When we are in the desert
and look up into the brilliant night sky,
we are looking into the Heart of God,
and each star is an "I love you" for humanity.

Each soul has the promise of being
a star in the universe.

Every voice has the potential
of being a note in the Symphony of Heaven.
For the music of the stars
is a work in progress,
a creativity that is never ending
to the glory of God.

Soul Whispers

In the desert the wind whispers quietly. Soul whispers that can only be heard once the mind has been stilled of all its questions, worries and ponderings. For God's voice speaks from the depths of eternity and eternity is only perceived through silence. The silence of the desert. It is there that the well of the soul is replenished with the waters of wisdom and creativity, for God's love is the very fountain of creativity. When you find yourself in the desert, take time to listen to the soul whispers, for they will lead you to an oasis; they will guide you out of the desert. To know the direction in which to travel one must first find the self in God, for He will lead you to eternity, to the treasures of the universe. He will lead you to the embodiment of love.

Light Friendships

Light friendships are forming in my life
like cottony clouds in the sky.
I ride those happy white wisps
seemingly higher and higher,
like friendships carrying me
one after another to Heaven's front door.

For years I've treaded on the rocks of the earth
thinking their heaviness was mine,
destined from birth.
Drama to drama I've been accustomed to,
believing they substantiated my worth.
But now I have these light little friendships
that bring me happiness and mirth.

For sure I want to wish both the people
of the drama and the light-hearted stories
an unfettered journey to Heaven
and all its glories.
I want them with me to imagine
huge invisible angels' wings to guard them,
to comfort them, to fly them free
throughout earth's domain
and remind them that one day
when all is said and done
those wings will unfold
and glide them with love
to God's Princely and Glorious Son.

Putting Wings on Souls

If we could look past the color of the flesh
or the shape of the face,
if we could get past the anger, the hurt, the disgrace,
if we could look into each others' souls
we could look into the heart of God
and the commonality of the human race.
If we could look at each others' souls in the light
we would see each other's gift of birthright
and we would be putting wings on people's souls
to soar above the pain of the earth
and save people from savage hell's gate.
If we had the patience of Heaven's realm
we would be putting wings on peoples' souls.
We would fly them from the poverty of the earth
to the abundance found in people's dreams
of rivers filled with milk and honey
of streets paved with gold.
We would put wings on people's souls
and fill them with the hope
that for ages has been foretold,
the rich would share with the poor
and treasures would be at every door,
for we would be putting wings on every soul.

Angels in the Making, or The Wings I See

The wings I see on people are the wings of the soul. Earthly wings are not angels' wings. They are the wings that become angels' wings when we enter Heaven. These earthly wings change with the nature of the soul. They grow in stature and beauty as the soul becomes more noble. Likewise, they become small and a caricature of what they are meant to be when the soul expresses petty behavior, contention, bitterness, and greed. We are all angels in the making, and when we see those with ridiculous wings, it is our job to nurture them back to wings of noble stature. For God has a place reserved for each individual in His Heart, and as angels in the making, it is our wish to ensure that God's Heart is filled with the special and unique love of every soul... a tribute to God for what He has sacrificed for us... the freedom of choice. The autonomy of free will, to live, to learn. To love. A piece of what makes God Who He is.

Sweet Song of Heaven

The phrase "I love you" is a song.
The sweetest melody comes from God

Life's breath, you are so sweet.
Of thee I wish to eternally eat.
Only by God's grace
do I savor thy fruit.
His promise to taste Heaven's air
has taken root.

Each breath we take
is an "I love you" from God,
and His "love you"
is good for all eternity
and fills the air of Heaven.

When we cross the threshold
and journey to Heaven,
not a breath shall be misplaced
nor shall the heart skip a beat.
For instantly we'll be there
in the midst of God's heavenly air.

Sweet song of heaven,
I'm glad that God does care.

The Abode of Angels

Beyond the darkest night,
beyond the farthest star,
there is a light that shines
that none may see,
save for those who have crossed
the threshold and made the journey to Heaven.

It is the abode of angels,
where the dreams of souls come true
and glory with all its brilliance
is given to God.

It is there that time has no meaning.
For all are in the presence of God
and live in the eternal now, ever awake
to the music of the spheres, the sound of
the universe, where angels sing their
most beautiful and mightiest song.

For none to hear but the Ear of God.

The Glorious Voice of God

The stillness of the universe is punctuated by
the sound of God. His voice singing "I love you"
in an infinite number of ways. Resounding
through the angels. Resounding through all of
life. Touching every corner of space. His
sound fills all of existence. Symphony to the
stars, Music of the Spheres. God's voice is
the Holy manifestation of love, an ever-
increasing touch of His Soul.

Do I hear the cry of the doves? Or is it the
murmur of angels? If only my soul could
listen more closely, maybe I could hear the
voice of God.

This Unrequited Celestial Love

Lord, would that I could be a balm for Your
sadness, the unrequited love. There are
those who would love You twice over and
twice over that to make up for those who
don't return the love You have for them.
I pray for the time that not an ounce of
sadness takes form in Your Being. That
happiness and joy fill You up in the love
You receive from Your Creation.

Dear God, with my prayer I give You the
hope that is in my heart.

"It is in the making of the Music of the Stars
that My happiness is complete."

A Trembling in the Land

Lord, You come to me
as a trembling in the land
till it deafens my ears.
Yet You are a soft whisper
in my soul.

Your Sound fills my being.
It runs through my limbs.
It is a joy to my body.
Your Sound runs through
the fabric of the universe.
All are touched
by the power of Your Voice.

Hail the Mighty God.

Hail Yahweh.

Trees

The imperfections of the world
are the rough soil out of which
grow mighty trees of love and
beautiful flowers of compassion,
generosity, and kindness. For sure
there are places that are barren on
the soil, but just one noble majestic
tree of love makes life worthy of the
imperfections and wonders of the world.

Diamonds in the Rough

As the souls of mankind, we are all diamonds in the rough. It is
the love of God and our love and caring for one another that are the
cutter's tools for shaping us into the brilliant facets that reveal the
jewel of Christ that is within us. Thus we must look at people as
the potential of shining with the Divine Light. Everyone has the
value of a jewel from Heaven within them. The irregularities and
imperfections of greed, avarice, prejudice, power, want, hate, and
lust are only the worldly disfigurements that we must attend to,
must recognize, so that we can stand before the Jeweler of Love
and be shaped into our true beauty, worthy of a place in Heaven.
The cross that we bear is the pressure that turns our souls into
diamonds. It is the careful craft of Love that makes us brilliant.
The Church on earth is a living diamond in the rough working to
reveal the jewel of Christ within.

The Souls of Mankind

Our souls are the prisms for
The light of God.
We all put forth different rainbows
Of color,
According to the nature of our souls.

As long as we keep our souls clean,
We can take part in beautifying
The universe.

For the universe is meant to reflect
The beauty of God.

By His grace we are the
Twinkles in His eyes.

We are the stars
In reality.

Lights in the universe
Of history.

Embers in the fire
Of hope...
We are the souls of mankind.

Mary, save for your Son Jesus,
Your colors are the most brilliant,
Most beautiful of all mankind.

The Brilliance of Your Love

Lord, You are the Fountain of Creativity.
You are the Spring of Wisdom,
River of Compassion,
Ocean of Love.
You give meaning to life,
reason to breathe,
and existence the desire
to be.

God, You are the Beginning and the End.
Transcending both time and space,
You go beyond the finite
and Your Being extends
beyond the doors of eternity.
I try to grasp You,
but my mind is not enough.
Yet You hold me in the cup of Your Hand
and lift me to the brilliance
of Your Heart.

Dear God,

Your love fills me up
as no other love does.
It is a comfort to me.
Your love lifts me out of the pitfalls of life
and up into clouds of wonderment.
When I hear you say the words "I love you"

I feel those words sink into the depths of my soul.
For surely Your love has been a constant for me,
and it is only the inconsistencies of my life
that prevent me from realizing the full magnitude
and scope of Your love, the love that abounds with no end.
Thank You for loving me.
For Your love, I pray that love be returned
to You in innumerable measure,
that You may feel what I feel from Your love.

My Soul Grows Young

I am one being,
both body and soul;
yet as my body grows old
my soul becomes younger
till my spirit touches God
and my body returns
to the ground.

My flesh becomes wrinkled with age
even as my soul becomes
more resilient, pliable, and free.
It learns once more to soar
again in timeless eternity
where it is winged as a child
amongst Heaven's angels.

So even as time weighs heavy
on my joints, muscle, and bone,
my soul grows closer to what
once was home.

My soul has an entire lifetime
to learn how to be young,
to play amongst the clouds and stars,
to ride moonbeams and sing with quasars,
and to rest with confidence and comfort
once again in God's heavenly arms.

(Inspired by Matthew 18:3)

The Journey, the Reward

Jesus, by His birth, started this world
on a spiritual journey. A journey
sometimes filled with danger and
hardship, sometimes with great
victories and joy. Those who don't
lose sight of the goal,
the destination, will be awarded the
treasures of Heaven and the
company of God.

The Road of Bliss

Life is mundane
punctuated by
moments of
happiness and joy.
Acknowledging
their ultimate Source
leads one to
the road of bliss.

Embraces

I have watched people hug each other. Friends, acquaintances, persons in my life who seem to be so carefree and easy with their lives. And I feel that I want to hug, too. But my timidness prevents me. So I send them a hug from my soul and hope that on some level they feel my heartfelt embrace, an embrace of friendship that lasts into eternity. For the people I would most want to embrace are the people I want to see in Heaven...

I would want to see you in Heaven.

His Song Resounds

Listen with your heart to that song.
Listen with your heart to the voice of God,
For God wants you to hear His words,
The words, *I love you.*
And when you hear those words
with your heart,
you join that community of people in the world
who hear those same words.
An *I love you*, a love that is placed in the heart,
that cannot be contained but is driven
to be shared with all beings on the planet
to ensure that the community grows and that love
reflects back to the glory of God through all nations
so that here on this sphere called Earth
His song resounds with all the joy and healing
that is graced in the Music of the Spheres,
notes in the Symphony of Heaven.
Give glory to God, listen with your heart
and share the love He places there.

The Sanctus

Our bodies are only vessels.
What we do with them,
how we act in the world
reflects how our souls
respond to the song inside.

A song placed there by God,
Who wants us all to hear
the Music of Heaven.

It is the Sanctus,
the music of peace.

Calmness comes to those who hear it.
Anxiety lifts from their beings.
Those who don't listen to it
are at discord;
war is in their midst.
Only by listening to the song
can peace be brought to the world.

God lifts His Voice
and sings throughout
the universe.

To Hear God's Silence

To hear God speaking to us is a joy.
But let us not fail to appreciate
the quiet moments...the silence of
His love, where we experience the
stillness of eternity and the rejuvenation
that comes from the peace that passes all
understanding. Even when God is quiet,
His love still sings to us. Let us not forget
to open our hearts so that we may hear His song.
Do not be troubled if God is still.

Silence is the empty canvas
upon which God's infinite wisdom
is written.

The Killing Fields

My life has been a dream,
and just now I am awakening
to my future.
God is the morning sun
warming every aspect of my life
to the promise of a new day.
This is the greater reality,
the meaning of my existence
to journey through the meadow of the world
with the light of God's love in my heart.

I walk through the killing fields,
and wherever a tear has been shed
or a drop of blood has fallen,
His compassion gives rise to
a flower of love
and the hope for a new world,
and a sorrow forgotten.

I walk through the killing fields
and realize healing
can only take place
through the might of God's Power
placed in our hearts.
Only His Love
can give life to the dead
and meaning to the suffering
that we all have led.

His Love, His Heaven

We experience life from moment to moment.
There can be, between each moment,
a place where someone expresses love to you
with all their intent and you open yourself
to that love with all the fullness of your heart.
An instant in-between time
when you see a beautiful sunset
and realize the grandeur of God.
Or when you look up into the night sky
and see the stars touching the infinite universe.
These are all instances where our souls
connect with eternity
and we get a glimpse of Heaven.
For God would not make a heaven
to hide from our senses
or keep from our knowledge
a place called Paradise;
rather He would give us a taste,
He would say, "This is what I have waiting
for you. For I have made you to enjoy
My Love, My Paradise, My Heaven."

A Tribute to God

A Tribute to God

Beyond the farthest star and the longest emitting light from this universe where time, matter, and energy turn back on themselves to gather for the next cycle of this universe, lies naught but the Being of God. Within His absolute State of Grace are the infinite multi-universes and heavens without end; His love ever sustaining Creation in all its forms, giving His infinite attention on every being in existence. And all He seeks is love... love from the creatures He made from the Power of His Word. Would it be too much that one sphere in His creation sing out a resounding "I love You" back into His Being? Could that sphere be Earth? Should not all people on this planet conspire to show our gratitude for life? To unite together not for the sake of defending against a common enemy, but rather to unite for the sake of love in celebration to God. What is Heaven on Earth except a tribute to God? Sing out an "I love You," share it with others till all on the planet sound out with gratitude to the Universe.

To the Reader,

I cannot fathom another person's relationship with God. Everyone has his or her own valid experience or non-experience with Him. It's just that when I see others and myself-display the lesser human characteristics, I want so much for a nobler demeanor to take place. We all have a spiritual nature intrinsic in our beings, one that recognizes both the joyful and the hurtful parts of humanity. It is when we are mindful of God that our negative aspects recede into the background of our behaviors. We all connect to God at some level, and no matter what level that is, it can be deepened and broadened. Our connection with God is a living connection. It can diminish or grow with our responses to the events that take place in our lives.

I must remember not to take for granted the love God shares with me. It is very special, as is the love He shares with every individual. It is not my place to compare how He shares that love with others or how apparent it might be with them. God's love is very personal and there are as many ways of experiencing that as there are people on the planet. To share in those experiences and the richness of His love is the ideal worship. It is how we grow and better ourselves in the wonder and awe of His creation. We are imperfect creatures and for the most part are only mindful of God from occasion to occasion. I pray we all grow more mindful of God according to our natures and that the peace and love of that practice touches all we know.

André L. George

About the Poet

I was born in Leiden, the Netherlands, on September 9, 1955, and came to America in 1960 with my parents. I spent my school years in Portland, Oregon.

In 1975 I joined the U. S. Army and served with Special Troops in Berlin during the 1976 Bi-Centennial. While in the service, I became afflicted with mental illness and suffered the insanity of schizophrenia and numerous hospitalizations until 1993, when I was introduced to what is for me the "miracle" drug Risperidone. The drug and prayers brought me out of my mental anguish and fears.

I am now working on personal issues, social adjustment and my writings. I now take comfort in my friends, my poems, and the Spirit of God.

André Leonard George
August 26, 2003